Terrance, * Happ[...]
You make us so ver[...]
love you Son!

[...] mom.

Dec 29, 2018

GOOD NEWS BUSTER

ON THE SOUTHERN PATH TO PURPOSE

THAÏS SHERELL

This book is a special gift. It
tells the story of your cousin
"Buster" (Babe's Brother) Enjoy!

Good News Buster: On the Southern Path to Purpose

Print ISBN 978-0-9814774-8-0
Library of Congress Control Number: 2018913100
Nonfiction > Biography & Autobiography > Historical
Nonfiction > Biography & Autobiography > Cultural Heritage

*Dedications *

This book is dedicated in memory of my Johnson-Brown ancestors who have provided a solid and rich legacy.

Special thanks to my uncle who has willingly and graciously allowed me to share his story which has been so inspirational to me.

Mom, thanks for being the portal for which I entered such an amazing family and for being a phenomenal role model.

To my children, siblings, and extended family – thank you for your never-ending love and support. May this book remind you of the greatness in our DNA.

To each reader - thank you for taking the time to be inspired by those who have inspired me.

And above all, thanks to my heavenly Father who gives me purpose for living.

FOREWORD

BY GARY GIBBS

Good News Buster chronicles the evolution of a young Baldwinesque character whose every step, like the writings of Teilhard de Chardin, flows toward that point, where there is a convergence with the Divine.

Buster's quest takes him from South to North, from church to stage, from sight to blindness and back again. Like the Saul/Paul saga and all the other proverbial blind men whose paths intersected with the merciful and loving God, Thaïs Sherell takes us to that epiphanous moment when Buster's calling eclipses his desire for fame. She bends time, like a Dr. Who episode, and takes us back to a season when the center of the Black community was the church.

Buster's unrelenting search brings a fresh biographical narrative to Mark's gospel as he swirls in sight and blindness, and bright lights and soul reckoning to ultimately bring us good news.

Search me, O God, and know my heart: try me, and know my thoughts: And see if there be any wicked way in me, and lead me in the way everlasting.

— *PSALM 139: 23, 24 KJV*

GOOD NEWS 1

There was no doubt about it. I was born to share the good news; I just wasn't sure how.

It was in Sumter, South Carolina on the twenty-sixth Sabbath of the year 1939 that I was born into this world. The times were both good and bad. Slavery had ended but riding on its heels were the Great Depression and World War II, making jobs even harder to find for people of color. And since Theodore Roosevelt – our 26th president – and Franklin D. Roosevelt – our 32nd president, seemingly helped people of color, I was given the name Roosevelt Johnson at birth.

Roosevelt was an honorable name indeed; yet, for some reason Mama started calling me Buster.

Buster was a catchy nickname which caught on instantaneously among my family and childhood friends. Eventually, I too favored the nickname because it made me feel extra bold and determined – *Buster defies racism, poverty, and anything else the South delivered.*

Initially, the thought of me busting down walls was somewhat comical because both my paternal and maternal grandfathers were Baptist preachers in South Carolina. Dad's father was Anthony Johnson; we called him Papa Johnson. Papa Johnson was a resourceful preacher who built his own church from the ground up, using wood chopped from trees on his land. His church was called Wilson Grove Baptist Church. Mama's dad was James Brown; we called him Papa Brown. I don't recall if he built his own church or not, but his church was called Jordan Chapel.

Going to church was a delight. It enveloped my childhood and I loved it! When we went to church, I sat close to the pulpit so I could see and hear everything. I took in every word as I watched my grandfathers open the holy book and proclaim the message of the Lord. As I listened, I imagined how one day I would do the same.

In addition to the spoken Word capturing my attention, there was Richard Johnson, my dad. He had an acapella gospel group that sang at my grandfathers' churches and often conducted the rehearsals at our home. This was always a special treat for my siblings and I because Dad was a self-made businessman who often spent long hours away from home.

Church folk loved when Dad's group sang. Dad was the group's time-keeping and melodious bass singer. Boy could he move the room with his low – low – low notes. When Dad's group sang, some folk clapped their hands, some folk tapped their feet, and some folk added to the joyous sound with the scrapping of wire on a washboard.

The words in the songs that they sang resounded the good news of God from East to West and from North to South. And when folk listened, they somehow knew that God's love and grace would help them in good times and bad times.

I knew then, as I tapped my small feet and clapped my small hands, that I too would have a gospel group one day. And, when God called me to begin it, I'd be somewhere listening for my name.

GOOD NEWS 2

Pecan-colored and peacock proud, I realize that growing up in the 1940s and 1950s had its perks, and it wasn't just because heavyweight boxing champion Joe Louis was whipping butts of all colors in the ring, giving people of color something to be proud of.

This "Brown Bomber", as he was known, rose up from the ashes like nobody's business. And like Papa Johnson's dad, Joe's dad was a sharecropper, gleaning food and splitting the spoil. Didn't matter none because Joe's past couldn't hold him down; he went from amateur to World Heavyweight Boxing Champion and stayed there over ten years.

Joe did us proud and made my childhood memorable, but he wasn't alone on that platform; there was something else that made my childhood memorable, school.

I attended Stonehill Elementary School in Sumter. Every day we had prayer, Bible study, and sang songs about the goodness of the Lord; these activities were a part of the day called Devotion. I loved Devotion because I got to do two of my favorite things – study the Bible and sing the good news.

Something about having the good news at school made learning wonderful. And like one of Mama's buttery biscuits on a plate of chicken liver, grits, and homemade gravy, I sopped up everything I was taught. I learned so fast that my teacher skipped me from first grade straight to third grade.

Now even though having your child in a class with older students has always been a concern for some, it wasn't for Mama. She was okay with it. No one was going to take advantage of me; I could speak up for myself. Besides, being with older kids wasn't the problem. Fact is, like most kids, sometimes I was good and sometimes I misbehaved. For example, prior to being skipped, one day Mama told me to stay in the house while she went out for work. I heard her, but I just didn't listen.

After she left, I snuck out to play with two of my buddies. We decided to go by Munk's house and make mischief. Munk was a gal from school that lived up the road.

Sneakily we walked the trodden path. As we got closer, we heard the faint giggles of Munk and some other young gals. Moving closer, we saw they were playing house. They were so engaged that they didn't hear us. Great!

The creases in the corners of my mouth slid upwards as I turned to my buddies and declared, "Let's have some fun."

"Yeah," they agreed. "What should we do?"

"Kick that house down," I replied. Then I snuck close and kicked the first thing in sight.

"Buster Johnson!" Munk yelled furiously as her hands closed tightly.

My buddies and I didn't hang around to watch if the other gals responded; we took off running. I don't recall which one did it, but one of the gals picked up a brick and threw it. Bam!!

"Help!"

This time it wasn't one of the gals' voices I heard; it was my own voice, coming from deep within me. You see, one moment I was running under the blue sky, and the next moment I was on the dirt road and everything was dark.

✳✳✳

Darkness became an unwanted companion that clung to me like glue. When I had awakened, I learned that the brick hit my spine, a trauma that caused me to go completely blind within three months. *Blind?! I was just seven years old.* And to add to the misery, the doctor told Mama that I might never get my eyesight back. We just had to wait, hope, and pray.

Normally I might have gotten the switch for this stunt of disobedience, but Mama didn't beat or punish me. I guess going blind was punishment in itself. Not to mention there was the agony of the outside light. It hurt my eyes so bad. There were days that I refused to come from under the bed because the light burned like coals of fire beneath my eyelids.

So, there I was, home and in the house after all. Neither Dad nor Mama had enough money to send me to a school for the blind; so, for a whole year I stayed indoors, imagining what my friends were doing outside. That was pretty bad for an active boy, but at least I could still hear the good news being sung at home and church.

GOOD NEWS 3

After being totally blind, I had begun to see out of my right eye.

"I see that red dress you got on Kat," I excitedly claimed one day as the darkness began to produce an image. Kat was my older sister.

"You can?!" she inquired, speculating I might have been teasing. And, to make sure I wasn't pulling a prank, Kat kept holding different things in front of me to identify.

"What color is this?"

"Blue," I replied.

"What am I holding now?" she continued.

Kat was determined to unravel any mischievous plot if there was one. When she was convinced that I could see out of my right eye, she jumped and hooted before running to announce the news to the rest of the family.

When Dad, Mama, and the rest of the family heard Kat's announcement, all they could talk about was the miracle the Lord had performed, making a blind boy see. We didn't complain or murmur that it was only one eye; we were thankful. Seeing with one eye was better than being totally blind. Hallelujah! Now I could finally return to school.

Third grade had all the usual stuff, but what I remember most was the play at the end of that year. You see, every school year ended with a big play; it was something that everyone looked forward to, especially me after Mrs. Davis, my third-grade teacher, announced something that sealed the path I would take.

Mrs. Davis was a light-skinned woman of color who dressed really nice and drove a really cool Ford Mercury. Looking back, I wonder how she afforded such a car because in the early 1940s, a car like that would've cost

$916 if it were new, and the average yearly pay for people of color was around $400. Anyhow, I remember that Mrs. Davis was very kind and professional. She always wore her hair in a neat bun that was pinned up in the back of her head; and if I had to guess, I'd guess she was in her late 40s.

"Class," Mrs. Davis announced when lunch and recess had ended, "the lead for this year's play is Roosevelt Johnson."

"Me?" I asked, trying to keep from jumping out my skin.

"Yes," she responded and smiled.

I gasped. I could hardly believe it. Having the lead meant I would get to sing a solo. Boy, I could hardly wait to tell Kat. She got to sing solo one year; she'd be so happy for me.

GOOD NEWS 4

Well, the day of the play came and passed.

My family and friends were there to cheer me on. They said I gave a stellar performance. I don't remember every detail, but what I remember most was the feeling that I wanted to sing for the rest of my life.

I was so serious about singing that I started a gospel group at school called The Gleam Light Juniors. We were all around the same age, but I was properly the most outspoken one.

"Guys," I informed the rest of the group, "we have to practice, practice, practice."

Practice and hard work were things Dad declared was needed to do a good job, and I believed him. Dad had done many wonderful things in his life by working hard. For one, he started his own construction business which was rare for men of color at the time.

Anyhow, the boys listened and we gave ourselves over to practice, practice, practice, and by the time we were fourteen years old, The Gleam Light Juniors had sung during Devotion for all the classes in our school.

Finally, I was singing in a real group like Dad!

GOOD NEWS 5

Singing with The Gleam Light Juniors for different teachers and their classes was a blast. Everyone in the school knew us; you could say we were school celebrities.

I suppose it was great making a name for ourselves, but I really just wanted to share my passion for the good news with others.

Eventually my passion outgrew our audience. I wanted to spread the good news beyond school. So, at the age of fifteen, I joined an older group of boys called The Gospel Stars that was headed by a boy named Bud. The Gospel Stars were definitely a step up in the right direction, but it was short-lived. A year and a half after singing with The Gospel Stars, I heard a harmonious sound playing on WFIG radio that called out to me. And to really draw me in, the sound would echo again on WSSC radio.

It didn't take long for me to uncover the source of that sound; it was a group called The Golden Five. They were the hottest group in Sumter, South Carolina, and man were they good!

Since the town wasn't that big, it was easy to find out where The Golden Five was performing next, and I would be there.

The performance was all that I had expected; they didn't disappoint, and so, it was clear what I had to do next. Orchestrating myself backstage, I located the group and approached them.

"You guys are good," I said. "I'd like to sing with you."

"Is that right?" one of the members replied while looking me over.

"That's right," I answered.

"Well let's hear something."

"Ok."

Without hesitating, I straightened my shirt and began singing. Next, I began crooning like I saw my grandfathers do when they preached. I added a "Yeah–eah–eah –eah, woo Lor–or–ord," and ended with a resounding "hmm–m–m!"

"Man!" was all they could say. And just like that, I became a member of The Golden Five. And though everyone in the group was from Bishopville, South Carolina – fourteen miles away from my home – every week they came to pick me up for rehearsals and singing gigs.

GOOD NEWS 6

By 1957 new opportunities were opening for people of color, especially if they could sing, dance, or play sports.

Elvis Presley, who was on the top of the charts with "I'm All Shook Up," shared the limelight with contenders such as Sam Cooke and Harry Belafonte – men of color – who were now ranking on the top charts with "You Send Me" and "Banana Boat (Day–O)." Yes indeed, a new style of music was advancing! It had people moving and swaying, jumping and hopping. It was the token that moved colored musicians from the depressing South to the happening North.

Speaking of the North, a buzz in town was growing to a roar. Word had it that a local group went to New York City to perform at The Apollo Theater in Harlem and won third place. Now if you don't know, The Apollo was the place stars were made. Every week The Apollo hosted

Amateur Night, a show where new talent competed for the audience's applause. The more claps the audience gave a group, the closer they were to winning.

The saying was, "You ain't nobody till you play at The Apollo." I hadn't been there yet, nor had I been anywhere out of the South, but I believed it. Take James Brown, and I'm not talking about my grandfather, who supposedly got his big break in 1956 after performing on The Apollo. And before him there were Billie Holiday, Ella Fitzgerald, Jackie Wilson, Sarah Vaughan, Lena Horne, and Sammy Davis Jr; they were all colored performers who gained higher esteem after performing at The world famous Apollo Theater.

I just had to find a way there.

GOOD NEWS 7

As fate would have it, The Senators – a local Rock and Roll group – approached me about filling a vacancy in their group. They had plans to go North, but one of their members backed out.

Initially I was conflicted with the idea. After all, I came from a family of preachers. My roots were in the gospel; wasn't I next in line to share the good news with the masses?

Sammie – the group manager and one of the lead singers – made a convincing point, "If you wanna get out the Sticks, you got to sing what the folks wanna hear." *The Sticks was what people called the South because there wasn't much there but grass and sticks.*

For days my heart seemed to drag beneath my feet with the notion of singing Rock and Roll, but Sammie made sense, and I desperately wanted out of the South. So, in hopes of leaving the Sticks behind, I quit The Golden Five and joined The Senators – another five-guy acapella group.

The Senators was my first non-gospel group, and they were definitely better than those local cats the town was buzzing about. I'd stay with them for a spell, until they made it to the stage of The Apollo. After that I could always go back to singing good news; couldn't I?

GOOD NEWS 8

The Senators practiced day and night until our songs and harmonies were cemented together. Then we wrote a letter to The world famous Apollo Theater, asking for an opportunity to perform.

The year was 1957. Waiting for the response had our nerves in a pickle jar, but finally they wrote back. The Apollo informed us that they couldn't guarantee that we'd perform; first, we had to audition. No worries, we would audition for The Apollo. There was only one problem; we had to come up with the money to get there.

I told Mama about the big opportunity up North. It would only cost seventeen dollars to get a Greyhound bus ticket to New York City. She thought it was a great idea, but she didn't have the money.

"Don't worry," she assured me. "Ima get you that money if I have to borrow it."

Mama did just that. I don't know who it came from, but Mama borrowed the seventeen dollars for me to take the bus to New York City. And since Kat had already relocated to New York City as well, I didn't have to worry about a place to stay; I could always create a padding on her floor. Everybody headed North was welcomed at Kat's home. If she didn't have space, she'd make some. Now that's Southern hospitality.

I was all set, so once the rest of The Senators came up with money for their fare, we made an appointment to audition and off we went. Big Apple, make way for The Senators!

GOOD NEWS 9

The day of reckoning finally arrived.

The back room was filled with performers from all over, hoping to make their big break into stardom. I was awestruck. I had dreamt about this moment for months. We were actually in New York City and about to audition at The Apollo Theater located in Harlem.

Waiting with the other hopefuls, my palms were sweaty and my heart was thumping fanatically in my chest. My mind was no better; it flashed every nerve-wrecking image it could conjure as we waited to be called. I suppose it made sense; after all, winning could change our lives for good.

Putting my body at ease, the stage manager called us forward. Sammie reassured us that we had it in the bag, and I chose to believe him and be comforted. And though it now escapes my mind what we sang for that audition, the next words from the producer caused all of us to panic. Perhaps we were too confident because after singing two lines we were told, "Thank you. That's enough. Please wait over there." *Wait over there! There where?*

Shaking my head, I looked at Sammie, "What'd we do wrong?"

There would be no explanation, not yet. So, we walked over "there" and watched as others auditioned. Some performers made it through their entire act; others were stopped and sent "there"- good and bad performers alike.

It wasn't until everyone had auditioned that the performers sent "there" were called back to the stage to hear their fate.

"Senators, you guys are good," the producer said. "You can come back next week and we'll see if we can get you in."

That was it; apparently "there" was the place to be. We would have a chance to perform next week in front of a live Apollo audience!

GOOD NEWS 10

The days leading from the audition to Wednesday's Amateur Night rolled around like black molasses rolling down Mama's tree, slow but sure.

We didn't have money to buy anything fancy for the live performance, so we went to a local store and purchased similar shirts. To this, we adorned ourselves with black slacks and spit-shined black shoes. It was the best we could do.

What we lacked in money, we'd made up in talent. And talent was needed this night in front of Apollo's exciting, yet frightening audience. There was no room for error; we had to capture the live audience's heart from the moment we walked onto the stage.

I wish Mama could have been there; surely she would be our biggest fan, cheering in the background, admiring how far her seventeen dollars went. But, Mama couldn't make it; still, she sent all the love she could through the airway. Meanwhile Kat, and a host of other family members and friends that had previously migrated from the South, would be in the audience to cheer us on.

"Senators, you're up next," the stage manager announced, interrupting my thoughts.

"Got it," Sammie replied.

"It would have been great if we had more time to practice with the band", I thought to myself. Unfortunately, we only worked with them once. That was all the time allotted for each act.

Sensing the closing of the act before us, Sammie motioned that we should move closer to the stage's entrance. My hands started sweating again as I peered out to see a packed house; I had never seen so many people in one place before.

"Relax," Sammie said and patted me on the back. "We're good. We got this."

I took a deep breath in and let it out slowly.

"Apollo audience," came the host's voice, "let's welcome to the stage The Senators!"

We gave each other hi-fives, straightened our clothes, walked onto the stage, and rubbed the rock - Apollo's legendary "Tree of Hope."

"And where are you guys from?" asked the host, looking at our outfits.

"Sumter, South Carolina," Sammie replied.

"You hear that Apollo? Fresh from the Sticks," he joked. At that the audience laughed and my fear arose. Then he asked, "What you gonna sing for us?"

Sammie told him and the host signaled us ahead with, "Alright, the stage is yours."

Some people in the audience were still chuckling over his comment about the Sticks. But once the music began, we fell in step like The Temptations and the audience began clapping.

We loved the energy coming from the audience and the audience loved the harmony we produced. And by the end of that night, The Senators had won first place and were asked to return the following week.

GOOD NEWS 11

The second week was similar to the first and we slayed the audience again.

We defended our win, came in first place for a second time, and were invited to return for week three. It was happening! The Senators were off to a phenomenal start.

Much more relaxed now, and confident, The Senators showed up for week three. Perhaps we were over-assured about ourselves cause on the third week things went differently. A group from New Jersey called The Lovelocks entered the competition that week, and they were good. When they performed, they stole some of the love from the audience with their rendition of "Your Precious Love."

The pressure was on. The new guys on the block changed the game.

"Apollo," the host spoke over the screaming audience after the votes were cast, "this is amazing! This has never happened before in Apollo history, a tie between The Senators and The Lovelocks! We can't have this. There can only be one winner."

The other performers were sent to the side while The Senators and The Lovelocks stood next to each. A beautiful model, whose sole job was estimating the level of claps and screams, waved her hand above each group while the audience voted again; however, they would not relent. The applause for one group was equally as loud as the applause for the other. The tie could not be broken!

The competition was on. The Senators and The Lovelocks would have to return the following week and perform again; therefore, management strongly suggested that both groups choose a new song in hopes of avoiding another tie. Well, we had come too far; there was no way we were giving up our winning streak, a new song it would be.

"We gotta up our game," Sammie told the group. We needed a song from the top of the charts, something that would grab the audience and hold them captive. So, after contemplating song possibilities, we finally agreed on "One Summer Night" by The Danleers; it was risky, but it was the hottest song out there. We had to practice, practice, practice.

In our determination, we practiced so much that our lead singer, Clarence, lost his voice on the day of the performance.

"Man, I can't make those notes," Clarence whispered after being unable to hit a few of his notes.

"Oh man," I exclaimed, "who's gonna take his place? It's gotta be a pretty boy." After all, every group knew to put the guy with the sweet, soft voice and pretty face in the front so the girls could *ooh* and *aah*.

We deliberated awhile before deciding that Sammie would sing the lead. He knew the lyrics, so all we had to do was rehearse the dance moves a few times. And as a precaution, we decided to lip-sync as we practiced so no one else lost their voice before the show.

GOOD NEWS 12

We were a little concerned when we reached the Apollo that evening; after all, we just switched lead singers at the last minute.

Luckily, The Lovelocks performed first that night. And either they forgot or plainly disregarded management's suggestion to change their song. They hit the stage, performing the same song from the previous week, "For Your Precious Love" by Jerry Butler. When we heard that we knew the win was ours, or so we hoped it was.

"Apollo are you ready?" the host yelled, after The Lovelocks left the stage. "Here they are again, still fresh from the Sticks, The Senators!"

After chuckling at the host's on-going joke about the Sticks, the audience got quiet as we stepped on the stage.

This time we had our outfits together. We walked on stage in our white tuxedos. Man, we were dressed down to the T; we were sharp!

The Apollo band began to play and Sammie crooned, "One summer night, I fell in love" while we did a synchronized spin. The audience went crazy. A few women ran to the front of the stage in expectation of being serenaded by Sammie. He didn't disappoint. Sammie leaned closer as if singing to them only, "One summer night, I held you tight. You and I, under the moon of love, moon of love." By then, the audience was screaming so loud that we could barely hear ourselves sing.

Well, we won first place that night with no discrepancy. And since this was our fourth win, we were invited to sing on the Apollo stage with the professional acts; we were no longer "amateurs".

The world famous Apollo Theater had given us a shot and we took it. We signed an agreement that required we perform three times a day, opening for Little Willie John,

James Brown, and some other big shots. Yes, our little group from the Sticks was on the rise.

The guys were proud and content with this new life, but not me. I only sang this kind of music to get out of the South; my heart and first love was singing the good news. I was clear about that. So, after fulfilling our initial agreement, I decided to quit the band. The guys weren't happy about my decision, but they respected it. Fame or no fame, I had to return to the good news.

GOOD NEWS 13

By now, my parents had relocated to Philadelphia – the city of "brotherly love." I too relocated to Philadelphia and awaited new opportunities to sing Gospel; it didn't take long.

One night I took a stroll home after seeing a movie. As I was looking around, admiring the tall buildings, I heard a sound. It wasn't just any sound. It was the sound I'd longed to hear. I followed the sound to a little church on South Street where a group – The Southern Wonders – was singing before a small congregation. This was it!! This was the opportunity I was waiting for.

By the time I walked in the group had sat down. I sat behind them. Once I figured out who the man in charge was, I tapped him on the shoulder and said, "Uh, good evening sir. I'm Roosevelt Johnson. I'd like to sing with your group tonight." The man chuckled, looked me up and down as the others had done, and then whispered something to the rest of the guys. I watched attentively and waited for a response.

After a moment or two, one of the other guys turned around and said, "We don't know you."

Well, little did The Southern Wonders know, I was determined to sing with them. I tapped the man in charge again and said, "I want to sing." This time he chuckled and said nothing more.

The church service continued, and I waited patiently.

Near the end of the service the man in charge noticed I was still waiting, so he took the mic, pointed to me, and said, "This young man *really* wants to sing. Now, we don't know him, but let's give him an opportunity."

My heart leaped as I got out of my seat and walked over to the guitar player. "Give me a B–flat," I whispered. "I'm going to sing 'I'm Pressing On,' the Gospelaires' version."

The guitarist played and I began singing. After the chorus, I looked at the guitar player and said, "Advance it." So, he took the song up one key. I started to ad-lib like I was preaching, and the congregation got excited. When I finished, the man looked at me and said, "Man, you got to sing with us tomorrow night."

"Certainly," I replied. "Where and what time?"

GOOD NEWS 14

The next night I was on time and ready.

It was another small congregation. When I walked in, Willie – the manager of The Southern Wonders – saw me coming and began telling the people about how we met the previous evening.

"Here he is," Willie announced with excitement. "C'mon up." Then he whispered in my ear, "Do everything just the way you did last night."

It was really happening! I was doing what I loved, singing the good news in the North.

After that night I continued to sing with The Southern Wonders. Night after night and year after year we played at various places bringing the good news.

Eventually, I ran into one of the guys that I sang with at The Apollo; I found out the group had dispersed after I left and Sammie continued to perform on his own. I was sorry to hear that, but I never regretted my decision to return to the good news; it was truly my destiny.

GOOD NEWS 15

As time would have it, my eyes started troubling me again.

I didn't have money for any fancy surgeries, but around the age of twenty-one, opportunity knocked again at my door. An office in Philadelphia needed patients to test their new cornea transplant procedure. Basically, it was an experiment that could possibly give me full sight in both eyes or make it worse. Well, I did what any other poor, colored man would do; I accepted the opportunity.

After the procedure, my sight started coming back. And if you've never lost your sight before, you can't imagine the extent of my joy. Having my eyesight again reminded me of the miracles that were in the songs I sang and the sermons I heard as a young boy in my grandfathers' churches. I was a walking testimony and I wanted to tell the world about it, not on a stage, but from the pulpit.

Diligently, I began studying the Bible so that I could teach and preach with greater purpose. I wanted others to experience God's healing power.

GOOD NEWS 16

At one church where I frequently visited, I met a beautiful, light-skinned gal named Myrna.

She would always talk to me about the second-coming of God. Of course, I had heard about it before, but I never focused on it much. After listening to Myrna, I would go home, open my Bible, and search for myself. Wow! It was like a new revelation of something that was always there. God was coming back again and there were things people needed to do to be ready. After discovering this, I could never go back to singing alone. I had to preach God's word fully!

Meticulously ordering my steps, God placed me under a leader who ordained me to preach God's word. And knowing I would need a helpmate, I asked Myrna to become my wife and life-long companion. Together we'd make the perfect team.

Myrna agreed, and I was assigned to the role of Assistant Pastor at a church in Philadelphia; it was the church's intention to appoint me as lead pastor after a trial period. You see, the church was known for their music and naturally they were attracted to the gift of music God had placed within me. Little did they know, I had turned in my hymn book to preach. Though I was humbled by the offer, I didn't feel it was God's plan for me, and so I continued as Assistant Pastor, occasionally taking outside preaching engagements.

In the fullness of time, a Men's Day Service was scheduled at a church in South Philadelphia. It was to be a great affair with the presence of Philly's top officials and leaders, and they were contemplating who the main speaker should be. A member of the church suggested that they invite me to speak. They did and I accepted the engagement. I was humbled again. You see, the person who suggested that I speak had never heard me speak before. He didn't know me and they didn't know me, but God knew me and had clearly orchestrated that engagement.

The whole thing was amazing! I can still recall words spoken to me by one of the head deacons on the day I was to speak. He walked up to me and asked, "You're the minister for today?"

"Yes sir," I responded.

"Okay. Well, there are sixty-six books in the Bible; don't preach them all."

Some welcome that was; now I really was trembling in my shoes. But, when time came to preach, I opened the Bible like I had seen my grandfathers do so many times, and when I opened my mouth, God spoke through me like he spoke through Moses, a man in the Bible who also felt ill-equipped in the beginning of his ministry. And by the time God finished using me to bring the good news, the same deacon that admonished me in the beginning, closed out the service by speaking highly in my favor.

GOOD NEWS 17

Word got out!

My preaching at the Men's Day Service aired throughout Philly, resulting in the founder of Messiah Baptist Church calling to invite me to speak. I accepted; however, the day arrived and I had come down with the flu, so I sent Myrna on my behalf.

"The church is packed," one of the ministers told Myrna. "He has to come."

Long story short, Myrna told me what he said and I obediently got up, got dressed, and went to the service. When the service had ended, the founder confided, "I have a church in North Philly. I've been praying and asking God to lead me to the man that's His choice for that church. Will you go and speak before that congregation?"

"Certainly," I replied in all humbleness. And though the service was scheduled on a communion Sunday, and I was unsure how to conduct that service, God used me again. And liking what he saw and heard, the founder invited me to preach for the following communion Sunday as well.

God showed up again and my name was added to the list of pastoral candidates, and when the votes were cast, I was chosen to be the head pastor.

It was in my obedience to accept the role of head pastor of Messiah that God continued my steady advancement; and, as the church family grew, so did my natural family – Myrna and I had four children and several grandchildren that would help in the ministry and continue the proclamation of the GOOD NEWS!

ABOUT THE AUTHOR

In short, Thaïs Sherell is an "agent of change." She is a mother to two stellar, biological daughters, and a host of young ladies and gentleman throughout the world. She is a life coach, motivational speaker, entertainer, and a licensed educator who specializes in Language Arts and the Teaching of Students with Disabilities. Her credentials include, but are not limited to, a B.A. in English-Spanish from Skidmore College, and a M.P.A. in Public Administration from Baruch College.

Thaïs embodies a diverse array of skills from multiple sectors which she passionately showcases in all her projects. Her projects holistically combine education, business and spiritual guide posts to effectively bring awareness to community concerns and introduce alternative conflict resolutions. Among her numerous credits, Thaïs has written and produced television productions, stage productions, film productions, and magazine articles promoting healthy living in and after life's storms. Ms. Sherell is a spokesperson for arts-in-education, family preservation, community partnership and wholesome entertainment.

For other titles by Thaïs Sherell visit Amazon.com. You can also connect with Thaïs Sherell on social media at www.nspired101.com, www.facebook.com/nspired101, or on Twitter @TSJheart. For educational resources by the author, visit N-Spired's store at https://goo.gl/irvuP5.

REFLECTIONS

Everyone has a path and a purpose. What's yours?

Step 1: Find your purpose

> Consider the skills, gifts, and/or talents that have always come to you naturally. These things may have fueled your joy and peace as well as the joy and peace of others.

Step 2: Make steady the path for your purpose

> Take any means to learn more about your skills, gifts, and/or talents. This can be done formally and/or informally: traditional classes, online classes, workshops, podcasts, webinars, books, mentors, etc.

Step 3: Take steps on the path towards your purpose

> Consider where your skills, gifts, and/or talents can make a difference - your home, hospitals, shelters, schools, social gatherings, etc. - and inquire about opportunities to get involved and share.

If this *is* your path to purpose, as you continue to share, more doors of opportunity will start opening and with greater ease. If not, and it's a continual hardship, go back to *Step 1* and reflect again.

***

Never despise small beginnings or the voice resonating in your soul,
for it can play an integral part of your path to purpose.
- Thaïs Sherell

***

Made in the USA
Middletown, DE
20 December 2018